SMART WEBSITES IN MINUTES

A Step by Step Guide on How to Create Beautiful and Responsive Websites with WordPress

Modupe Salmat

This E-book is Dedicated to the Almighty
God and to my wondeful family

INTRODUCTION

Smart Websites in Minutes is an eBook that helps you in creating Beautiful and Visually Stunning Websites in Minutes. In this e-book you are going to learn how to use WordPress in creating beautiful websites for your online business as well as for clients. The eBook is created with non-techy people in mind. You are able to build websites from scratch without writing any single line of code using WordPress.

PREFACE

In this eBook, you are going to learn how to build beautiful, stunning and responsive websites with WordPress for your businesses and for clients

SMART WEBSITES IN MINUTES

A complete Guide on How to Build Beautiful and Visually Stunning Websites in Minutes

By Modupe Salmat

Legal Notice

CLICK HERE TO JOIN FACEBOOK GROUP
https://www.smartdropshippers.com

Table of Contents

CHAPTER 1, MODULE 1.

INTRODUCTION TO WEBSITE DESIGN AND
DEVELOPMENT

Differences Between a Blog and a Website

I will like us to start by first of all differentiating between a blog and a website. Oftentimes we take both terms to mean the same but they are not.

A Blog is a type of website that is regularly updated with new content while a website is static in nature and contents are organized in pages. Blogs can be part of a larger website. Some businesses have blog sections where they regularly create content to inform and educate their customers. You can use WordPress to create both a website and blog. Most Business owners use it.

WordPress is the simplest, most popular way to create your own website or blog. It is a content management system. A content management system is basically a tool that makes it easy to manage important aspects of your website without writing or knowing anything about codes or programming.

It's the best way to build any type of website *Features of a Professional Website*

A professional website must possess the following qualities

It must have an ideal domain name and must be put on a good host for fast loading.

It must have a nice and clean design.

It must have a clear navigation.

It must be responsive and have a mobile friendly version.

It must have nice looking images.

It must have a color theme

Contents must be above the folds.

Although, there are other features of a professional website but I will like you to see the above features as a checklist to every professional website you are going to be building for your clients.

And that takes us to the website we are going to be creating in this course

www.smartwebsites.smartdropshippers.com

This website is similar to the websites of big brands like

www.airbnb.com, www.nike.com www.uber.com
Why are they professional looking? Because all their contents
are above the fold! You don't need to scroll all the way down to
view their contents. Do you notice the navigation? Simple and
easy to navigate. And the headlines, sub headlines and the call to
action buttons as well as the full size image? All above the folds!
Big brands like Airbnb, Nike, Uber etc. create website like this
because websites with full screen image and call to action immediately people visit your site works! I will be showing you how
to design this website
(https://www.smartwebsites.smartdropshippers.co m) step
by step.
A glimpse into what we are going to be discussing are;
How to add the headlines, sub-headlines and the call to action
buttons?
How to add a full size image to your website
How to create and add your logo
How to create your navigation
How to add your social media buttons • How to add a contact
form to your site • How to customize your pages and lot more.

CHAPTER 1, MODULE 2
HOW TO CREATE A PROFESSIONAL WEBSITE STEP BY STEP

Remember the website we are going to be building together www.smartwebsites.smartdropshippers.com
If you can design the above website following this training step by step, believe me when I say you can design any type of website for people using WordPress.

There are four steps involve in designing a professional website

1. A Domain name
2. A Hosting Plan
3. WordPress Installation
4. Customizing Website pages like a Pro

A Domain name

A domain name is the name your website will bear on the internet. It can be any name. For example www.yourname.com. A good domain name will be the corner stone of your website's success. And that takes us to the qualities of a good domain name.
A good domain name must be;
Short and Catchy
Easy to Remember
Easy to spell
It has a .com extension
It is descriptive or brand able
It contains no hyphen or numbers

Another feature I will like to add is that it must cut across all social media platforms. It is a better idea if you can secure the name or have the same name for all your social media presence.
There is a tool you can use to check this out before purchasing the domain name and it is called namecheck https://namechk.com/
You will be able to check if the name is available, on what

extension and if the social media handles are available as well.

Web Hosting

Web hosting is a service that allows your website or web page to appear on the Internet. A web host, or web hosting service provider, is a business that provides the technologies and services needed for the website or web-page to be viewed on the web. Websites are hosted, or stored, on special computers called servers. When some-one visit your website by typing in your website address or domain into the browser, the person's computer will then connect to the server of your webhost and your webpages will be delivered to the person through the browser. How fast your website is delivered to your visitor depends on the reliability of your webhost or the hosting company you choose. The hosting company you choose may make or mar your business. It is advisable you choose wisely.

And that is why I always recommend Bluehost for your website hosting but if you are just starting out and you are on a low budget, you can try out Smartweb, they are tested and trusted!

With Bluehost, you get a free domain name, free ssl certificate, one click WordPress installation, 99.9% up-time, 30 days money back guarantee, easy to use Cpanel, a huge discount on hosting price, 24/7 support, superb customer service, and officially recommended by Word-Press.org. Using Bluehost is going to save you a whole lot of stress and money in the future

WordPress Installation

In this third step, we are going to install WordPress. WordPress is a contents management system that helps you manage all of your content files like text and images without writing a single line of code. It is use by professional web developers and it is the most popular content management system.

Customizing your website pages

This is the fun part! This is where we are going to be designing and customizing all of our webpages using a Plugin.

But first of all, let go over how much all these would cost.

Domain = $11.99/yr

Hosting = $10/Month

Wordpress = Free

Customizing Webpages =>> Free-> because we are going to be building the website ourselves and for clients, instead of paying web developer thousands of dollars in creating our websites.

As you can see, the only thing that would cost money is Domain name and Hosting which is step one and two. I have a discount for both steps with Bluehost . Also, if you are really on a low budget, I will advise you start with s-martweb because of their superb customers' service too but bluehost is the best if you can afford it.

So, let begin by registering a domain name and hosting with Bluehost.

Open another browser and type in www.bluehost.com Click on the "*Get Started*" button to continue.

On the next page, you are to choose a plan. You can choose the basic plan since you're just starting out.

Next, is to choose your domain name or link an existing domain name.

But If you already have a domain name from another hosting provider, you will need to link the nameserver of that domain to that of bluehost.

On the next page is to enter your details as shown in the image below;

On the next page, choose your package plan.
Either 12, 24, or 36months base on your choice.

The price reduces as the month you chose increases. The
rest of the boxes can be left blank.

Enter your credit cards details to check out on the next
page.

After that, scroll down and tick the *"Terms of Service"* to agree then finally click the submit button.

Congratulations! You just completed the first stage of your business website creation.

Install WordPress

Another great feature of bluehost is that wordpress is automatically installed for you while checking out during the course of your registration.

Immediately after submitting your details during checkout, you will receive a registration successful message and will also be prompted to create a password.

But first of all, go to your email address and click the confirmation link.

Click on the verify your email button.

After verification, go back to the create a password page to create your password

click on create password

Agree to terms of services and click on next.
Click the login button to login into your account.

Type in your site name and tagline.
Answer a short question about your website
Give little details about yourself
You can skip this step by clicking I don't need help
You will be prompted to pick a theme.

You can either skip this step or pick a theme.
When you skip this step, you will be presented with a
page like the image below;

Click on start building or go to your bluehost account.
On the bluehost client area click on login to WordPress.

Viola! You are in your WordPress dashboard.

Note: You will need to go back into your email to check for your cpanel username and passwords and make sure you save them in a notepad

Right now, your site is not visible to people. In order to launch your site, you need to hit that option on the top that says 'Coming Soon Active and click on launch site on the next page

To login into your WordPress admin dashboard go to www.yourbizname.com/wp-admin or via your Bluehost dashboard by clicking the *"Login to WordPress"* button to start customizing your website.

You can also login to your cpanel using your cpanel login details by tping www.yourbizname.com/cpanel on your browser.

For those that would be using smartweb or any other hosting company, you will need to install wordpress from your cpanel.

To do that, go over to your email to grab your cpanel login details.

Scroll down to softaculous App Installer/Quick Install Click on WordPress

You will be redirected to where to install WordPress
Click on install as shown in the image below.

Choose the domain you want to install WordPress on.
Name your site and type in the description

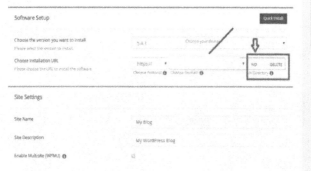

Scroll down to create a password then click on install.

Wait for it to install in few seconds.

Login into your WordPress dashboard with your user-name and password you created earlier.

If you have gotten to this stage, then you deserve a pat on the back. Well-done!

This is where we build our professional website.

So, let's go ahead!

CHAPTER 2, MODULE 3.
ACTIONS TO BE TAKEN BEFORE
CUSTOMIZING A WEBSITE

Before customizing a professional website, there are some actionable steps we would need to take right inside our WordPress dashboard. See these steps as checklists in building a professional looking website for clients.

Step one: **Change your Password**

This step is not compulsory but it is necessary for security reasons. To change your password, From your dashboard, click on users.

Click all users.

You will be redirected to your profile page.

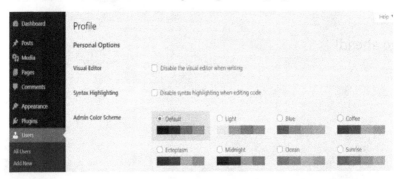

Scroll down to Account management and click on generate password.

Type in your new password and click on update profile.

Step Two: **Delete Unnecessary Plugins**

Plugins are additional features and add-ons to your website. By default, hosting companies get paid to install plugins on WordPress sites and that is why most of these plugins are installed with WordPress installation. Some of these plugins are not really necessary or they may not be useful to us so we would need to delete them in order to have a clean site.

To do that, click on Plugin on the left hand side of your dashboard.

Scroll to see all of the plugins installed with WordPress.

What we want to do is to get rid of all of these plugins. To do that;

Click on plugins

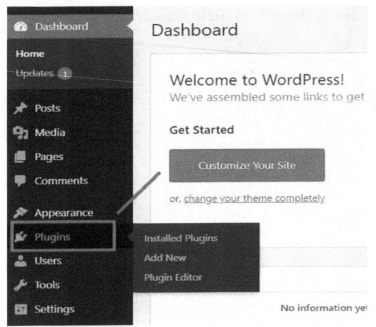

Click the checkbox in front of plugin.

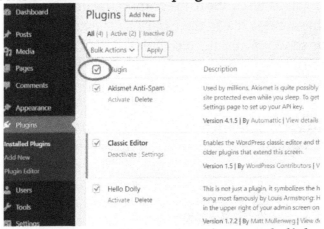

From the dropdown, click on deactivate and click apply to deactivate all of the plugins.

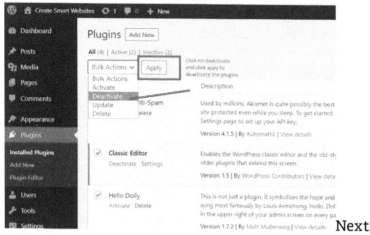

Next thing we are going to do is to delete the plugins To do that, click on the checkbox again in front of plugin.
Click the dropdown button and click delete.
Click apply and you are done deleting all of the unnecessary plugins.

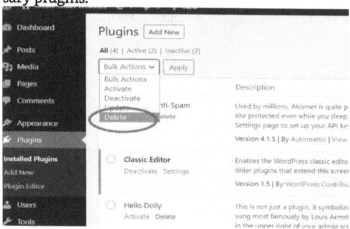

Step Three: Change Site Permalinks.

Permalink is the full URL you see on the search result when you visit any post or page of a website. Permalinks are an important part of your website because search engines and visitors use these URLs to index and visit your site. The type of permalink you pick determines the way these two parties see and value your site. Take for instance, when you visit your site and click on the sample post, what you see on the search result is your site permalink.

By default, WordPress uses a permalink structure that's not SEO-friendly and nonprofessional. And that is why we need to change it to have a more SEO friendly permalink.

To change your website permalink, go back to your dashboard

Go to settings.

Click on permalinks.

Click or check post-name.

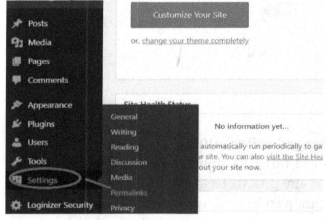

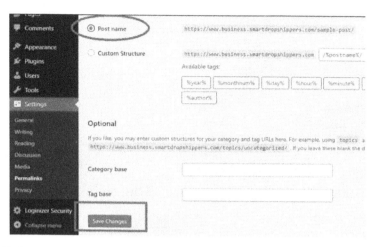

Click on save changes and you are done!

Step Four: Update WordPress to the Latest Version

Before building your website, make sure you are using the latest version of WordPress. Make sure your Word-Press is updated and it is with the newest features to protect you from hackers.

So to do that, click on update from the dashboard and your site will be updated after a few seconds.

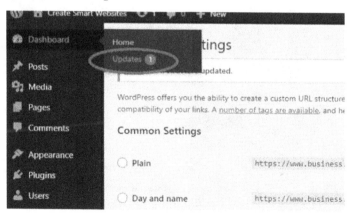

Then you will be presented with a page as shown in the image below.

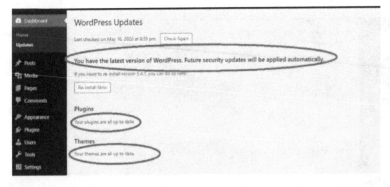

At times you may not have any update to do, so leave it and update any time you have to do so.

Step Five: **Install a Theme.**
A theme is the design of your website. One good thing about WordPress is that there are thousands of different themes to choose from and most of them are free.
To install a theme, go to your dashboard.
Click on appearance and then click themes

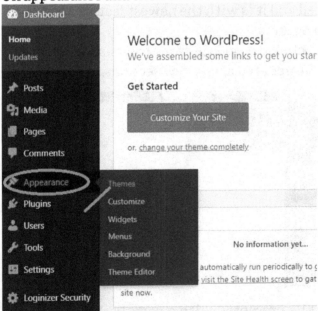

Of course you will see your presents theme and a couple of other themes but you can add more by clicking on add new.

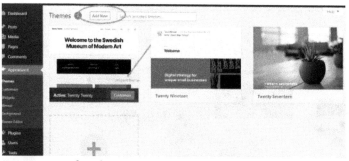

Once you do that, you will be able to see a whole bunch of different themes under featured, popular, latest, favorites and they are all free.

All you have do is to click on details and check the theme out.

To pick a free theme, make sure the designs and ratings are good. You can also preview each theme and you can install them by simply clicking install and activating any of them.

Also, if you have a theme in mind, all you have to do is to search for it in the search box and if the theme is a **premium theme** then you will need to upload it by simply clicking the upload theme button.

For the purpose of this training, we are going to be uploading a premium theme called Genesis Framework as well as a child theme (Daily Dish).

Why Premium Theme?

Premium WordPress themes are themes which have been professionally designed and coded with advanced features, functionality and additional services. A premium theme gives you more design options. You are able to customize it the way you like.

Note: Once you have the framework, you can download any genesis child theme on the internet. In this training, am going to be using the *Daily Dish Pro theme* which is a child theme.

If you are going to be choosing another child theme then your design will definitely look different from the one you have in this training manual but customizing genesis child themes are similar if not the same. So, follow the same process, to customize yours.

Click Here to Download the Themes.

To upload the themes, click on upload theme on the upper left area and it will redirect you to where your theme is being downloaded.

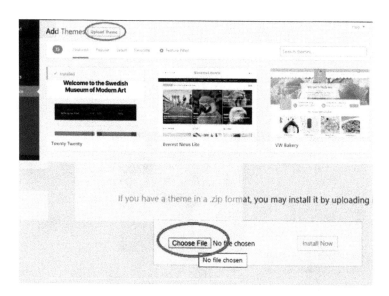

Choose the genesis framework theme first, install and activate it

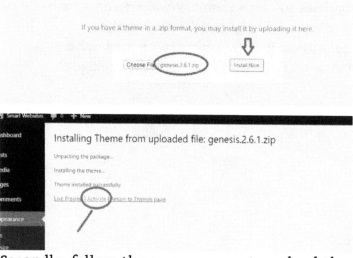

Secondly, follow the same process to upload the child theme, install and activate it.

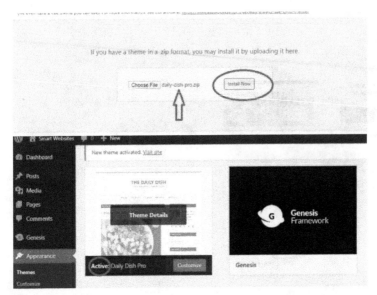

For this theme to function properly, we need to install two plugins. Remember, I said that plugins help in adding more functionalities to our website. We are going to install the *Genesis eNews Extended* and *Simple Social Icon.*

To do that, go to plugins and click add new then search for both plugins in the search box of Plugins, install and activate both plugins.

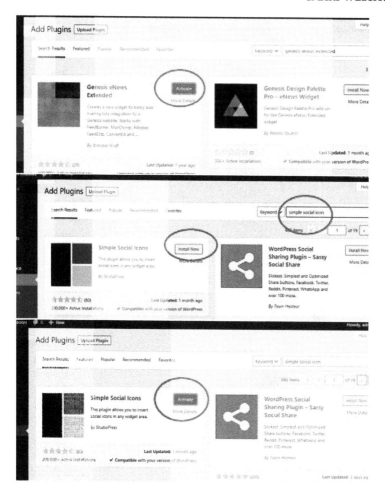

Click to view your website. You will notice that the look and design has changed.

Now that we have install a theme, let's move to the next step.

Step Six: Delete Sample Page

WordPress installed a sample page automatically that we need to delete. To do that, go back to your dashboard. Click on pages and select all pages.

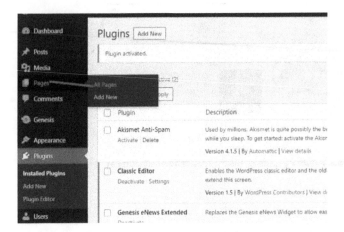

Click the sample page and select trash.

Click the trash button where the deleted sample page is being stored and click delete permanently to keep everything clean and organized.

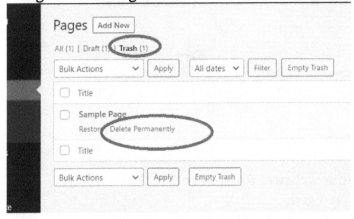

Step Seven: **Create Pages**

The next thing we are going to do is to add pages to our website. These are the regular pages like the home page, about me page, contact us page, services page, our work, blog page etc.

To do that, click on pages

Click on add new.

Type in Home and click the publish button.

Click add new to create about me page

Click on publish again.

Repeat this process by just typing in the page name until you finish creating all the pages you need. For the sake of this training, I will be creating the home page, about us page, our work page, services and contact page.

After creating your pages, view your website to see the changes you have made.

You will notice that none of the pages you created is showing and that takes us to the next step.

Step Eight: **Create Site Navigation.**

Navigation helps people find your contents and pages easily. To do that, click on customize from the top of your site.

When you do that you will be taken to a page as shown in the image below.

Click on menu.

Click on create menu

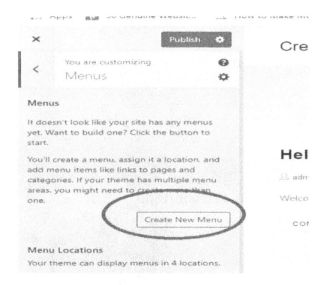

Name the menu and state where you want to display the menu.
Choose before the header menu or check both options.

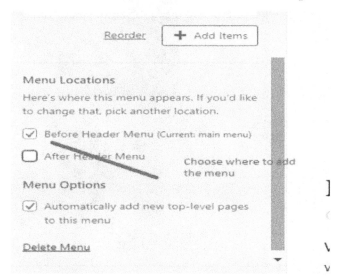

Click on next.
Click on add items to add the pages we created earlier

Click the plus button to add all the items.

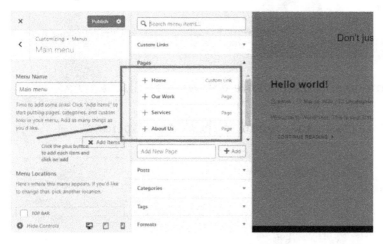

Then click on add items.

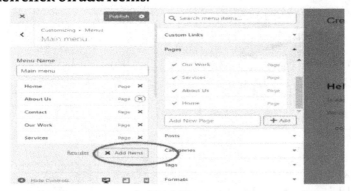

Once you click on add items, the navigation bar will be created as shown below.

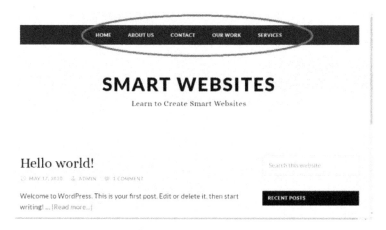

You can hold and drag to re-arrange the items. Also, if you would like to create a sub-navigation, you can hold and drag under any of the item to make it a sub menu as shown in the image below.

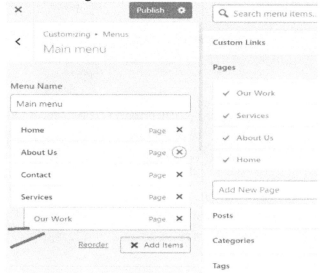

Click the back button twice to go back. The next thing we are going to do is to add an header image (Banner).

Click the back button twice and click on header image.

To insert our header image, we would need to design one quickly.

In creating our header image, we are going to be using a website called Canva.

Canva is an online visual editor. It's all drag and drop software for designing website banners, professional images, social medial headers, post images, email headers,logo etc and it's free.

To use canva in designing your logo and other websites essentials like images, banners, email headers, ebook covers etc. you will need to sign up for a free account.

Sign up for Canva here

Visit https://www.canva.com.

Click the sign up button.

You can sign up with your Facebook account or email

address.

Confirm your account and login.

Search for header image in the search box.

Click on custom because base on our theme requirement, we are to insert a header image of 400x80px (pixel).

Go back to canva and click on custom then insert the

header size in the box.

Click on create new design.

You will be presented with different frames you can use. Choose one base on the way you want your banner to look.

Click and drag any of the frames of your choice to the right hand side as shown in the image above or choose a template.

Click on upload on the left hand side to upload your images for the banner.

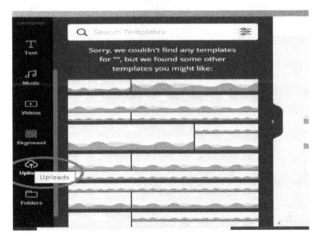

Change the color of the template to any color you want by clicking the color palate.

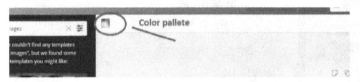

Change the image to your own image and add text to your design.

Click on download when you are done creating.

Now that our header image is ready, let's go back to our website and add it.
Remember where we stopped, as shown in the image below.

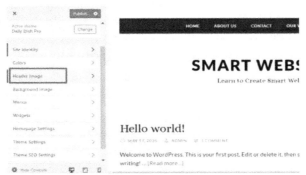

Click on restore auto save because all our customization has not been published so we will need to click on auto save in other not to lose them.

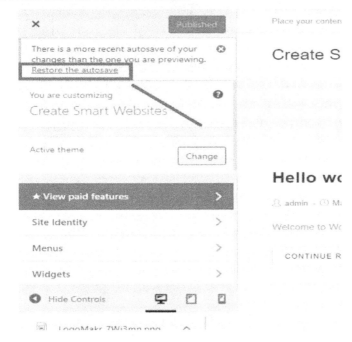

So to add our header image, click on header image.

- Click add new image.
- Clicking upload files.
- Click select files.
- Choose the header image from your desktop.
- Click open and wait for it to upload.
- Click on select.
- Crop or skip cropping.
- Click select media.

And we can finally click on publish to see all our changes. Click to visit the site and you will see that is looking awesome.

Although, instead of adding a header image to that space, we can actually add a logo but I think is good we add the logo "before the header" and what that means is that we can add the logo through a widget. To access your widget area, click on appearance from the dashboard.
Click on widget.

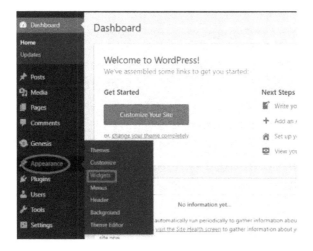

We can add the logo by placing the image widget before the header as shown in the image below.

- Click to choose the logo from your computer and click on save after uploading.

Now that we know how to insert our logo via widget, let's go ahead and design one for our website.

How to Design a Business Logo

A simple logo design can be done using a website called Logo maker or Canva.

Both canva and logo maker are great for designing logos but canva can still be used in creating and designing various things like ebook covers, banner, flyers, social media images etc. and it is free.

Click here to sign up for Canva.

Since we are only designing logo for now, we can quickly use logo maker which is another great website for logo design and it is also free.

Visit https://www.logomakr.com.

Type in the name of any shape in the search box.

For the sake of this training, I will just type in mountain. You can type in mountain, compass, flowers or any shape you like.

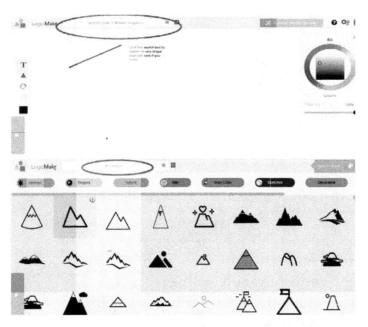

Pick any of the shapes under mountain by clicking on the shape and it will be added to the canvas.

You can click the corner boxes to resize the shape.

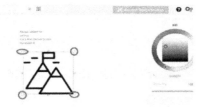

You can click on the logo itself to drag it around the canvas.

You can add text to your logo by clicking on the text icon on the left hand side and by typing in your business name.

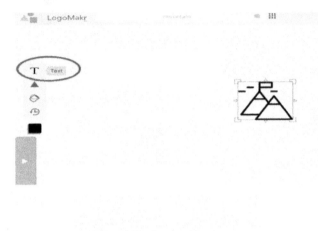

You can delete the text if you prefer icon only.

You can change the color of the shape or text if you want. To see the shape clearly, you can give it a black background and to do that, right click on the background and click "black background" or Transparent background depending on the color you choose.

To make your text and shape one, drag your mouse over them and they will be seen as one, you can then change the color to any color by just clicking the color palette.

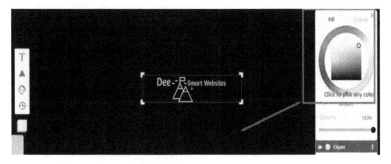

- Right click on the background and make it white again.
- Click on save on the right hand corner.

- Follow the prompt and click "No thanks".

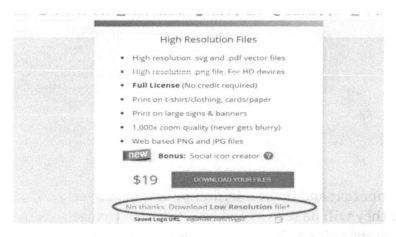

The logo will then be downloaded.

Go to where the logo is saved to rename it.

And we are done creating our logo.

Now that our logo is ready, let's go back to the website we were building and add it.

Remember where we stopped, as shown in the image below.

So to add our logo, go back to the site we were building.

- Click on appearance.
- Click on widget.

You will be taken to a page as shown in the image above.

Drag the image widget under the before header section.

- Click to add image.

- Click on upload files.
- Click on select files to select the image from desktop.
- Click on add to widget.

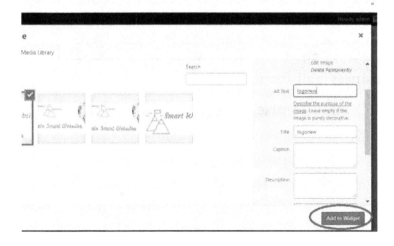

- Click on save.

Visit site to view our progress.

Your site should look amazing just like the image below.

Step Nine: Change Title and Tagline.

The next step is to change the title and tagline of our website. Tagline gives more information about what your site is all about. Instead of the default tagline "Just Another WordPress Site", you can change it to reflect what your business is all about.

To do that, click on customize.

- Click on Site Identity.

- Under Site Title, put in your business name
- Under tagline, describe your business

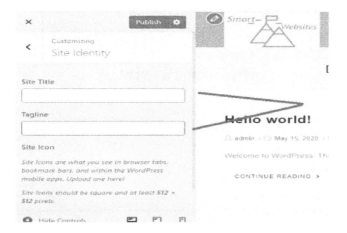

- Scroll down to insert your site icon (favicon) (Favicon is the small image that comes with every site on the search engine result).

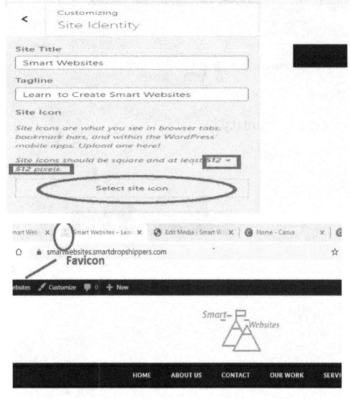

- Click save and publish at the top.

Step Ten: Setup Homepage.

As we can see from the image below, our home page is setup as a blog and that is why we are seeing the first sample post on our homepage each time we visit.

Hello world!

Welcome to WordPress. This is your first post. Edit or delete it, then start writing! ... [Read more...]

If you want a blog on your website, that is great but that is not our focus. Our focus is on building a professional website and that is why we will have to move the blog page to another page if we so wish to have a blog on our website.

To setup the homepage as a regular page. We are going to refer to the page we created earlier called "Home".

Note: Any page can be setup as your homepage but right now we want to make the page we created as home as our homepage.

To do that, click on customize from the top of the browser showing your site.

- Click on homepage setting.

- Check the box static.
- Choose home from the dropdown.

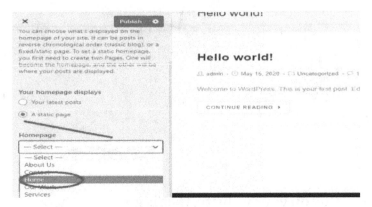

- Click on publish.

And we are done setting the page named home as the homepage.

Visit the website to view your progress.

It should look similar to the image below.

As we can see from the image above when we visit our website that both the homepage title and sidebar contents are showing and we need to get rid of those before we can start customizing our pages one after the other.

To get rid of that title and sidebar on the homepage, first of all, we need to install a plugin called "Genesis Title Toggle". To do that,

- Click on plugin.
- Click on add new.

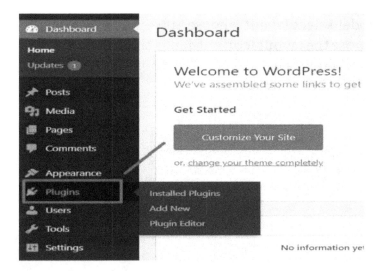

- Search for genesis title toggle in the search box.

- Click on install and activate the plugin.
- Click on edit page on the top of the browser showing your website.

- Scroll down to layout settings.

- Under select layout, choose 100% full width or choose the layout icon without a sidebar.
- Scroll down a bit and check the box "hide title" below the layout settings.

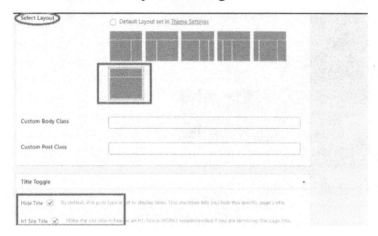

- Scroll up and click on update.

When you visit your website, you can see that both the title and sidebar are gone.

Your new homepage should look something similar to the above page. Everything is clear and clean for us to start customizing.

Step Eleven: **Customize Your Website.**

Customizing website is the fun part of any professional website. The old way of adding content is just to click on edit page and start adding contents. There is a better way of adding contents to our website which will make it more visual and make it look professional.

To start customizing our website pages, we will need to install a plugin called Elementor.

To install the plugin, go back to your dashboard.
Click on plugin.
Add new.
Search for Elementor in the search bar.

Click on install and activate the plugin.

Elementor plugin is one of the most advance page builders, used by professionals in building websites. You can do a lot with the free version of this plugin but if you need more functionality, you can sign up for its paid version.

Click here to check out Elementor Pro

Once your plugin is installed then we can start building our pages with it one by one.

CHAPTER 3, MODULE 4,
HOW TO CUSTOMIZE THE HOMEPAGE

Having installed elementor page builder plugin. The next thing we are going to do is to change the font in elementor as well as the theme font.

It is important to note that elementor plugin will only affect the body of each page you intend to design but not the header, footer, blog pages or shop page of your website. If you use elementor to design a page, you will need to change the theme font of that page for the header or footer of the page to have the same font as the body content of the page built with elementor.

So to change the font for elementor, from each page you intend to design, click edit page.

- Click edit with elementor.

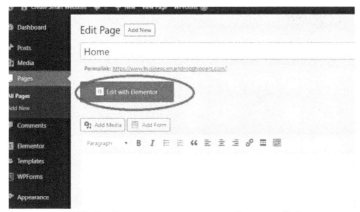

- Click the very top menu item of elementor page builder on the left hand side of the page you are designing.

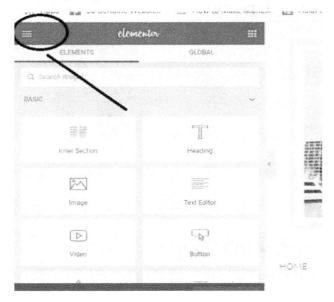

- Choose global or default font from the list depending on the version of elementor you installed.

You will be presented with a page as shown in the image below.

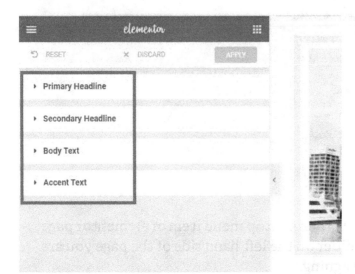

- Click on each headlines and change their font family to "Roboto or Lato" and leave the weights the way they are.

- Click apply at the top to save changes.

The motive behind this step is to keep everything consistent.

To go back to your dashboard, scroll down and click "exit to dashboard" at the bottom of the page.

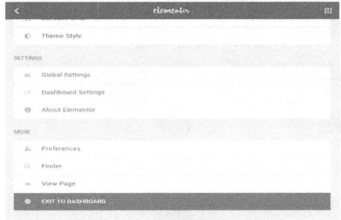

To set the theme font, we will need to download a plugin called google font.

- *Follow our previous lesson on how to install plugins, install and activate google font plugin.*
- After installing and activating the plugin.
- Go to the dashboard.
- Click on customize.

You will be presented with a page as shown in the image below.

- Click on google fonts and you will be presented with some options.

- Click on Basic settings and change the font family to roboto or lato.

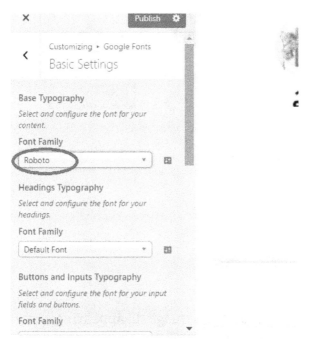

- Click each options and change them to roboto or lato then click save and publish.
- Go back to your home page and click edit page.
- Click edit with elementor.

Note: You could see that instead of giving us a clean page to design, the header image is not allowing that. It is showing. So we will need to get rid of it.

To do that click on appearance from the dashboard and select header.

- Click hide header image and click on publish.

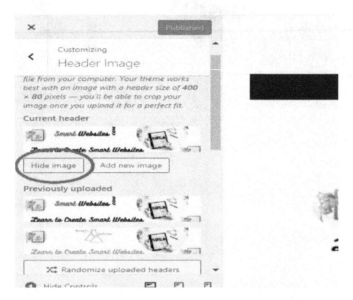

We can see that instead of the image disappearing completely, it was replaced by some texts.

So we will need to remove it manually using css.

Trust me, this is very easy to do so don't be scared! To do that, visit the website in another tab.

- Right click on the site and choose inspect from the list.

You will be presented with some lines of codes below the page.

  • Click the cursor icon on top of the code page.

  • Click the cursor tool and place it on the header text (Title and tagline) to know the name of that portion.

That give us the code that is holding the title and tagline text which is header.site-header.

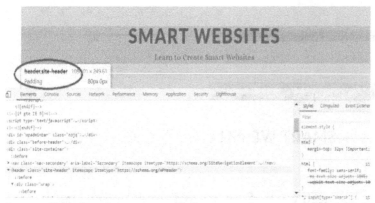

Immediately the name of that portion appears, click on it.

Its corresponding code will be display on the right hand side of the page.

In front of the code, press enter key on your keyboard and type in display:none.

That is, the site header should not be displayed.

Copy the three lines of code and go back to your CSS file.

To do this click on Appearance.

- Click on customize.
- Scroll down to additional css.

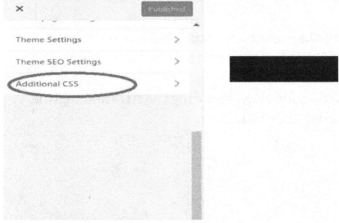

- Paste the code you copied there and click on publish.

If there is an initial code there, delete and replace it with the one you copied.

If you can't trace the code, just copy and paste the following lines of code below in the additional css portion and click on publish.

.site-header
Padding: 80px 0;
Text-align: center;
Display: none;

View the page and you will see that the texts are gone.

To start building each page with elementor plugin is very easy to do especially if you already know how to build pages. All you have to is to import templates into elementor or use elementor inbuilt templates.

- To import templates, click on templates from your dashboard.
- Click on saved templates.
- Click on import templates at the top and then choose the file from your computer.

Another great feature of elementor is that you can create a template and re-use it on any other website.

To do that, click on add new template instead of importing template from the top.

- Choose the template type and click on create templates.

It will redirect you to elementor page editor.

- Click the add template icon to see different elementor templates.

Drag widget here

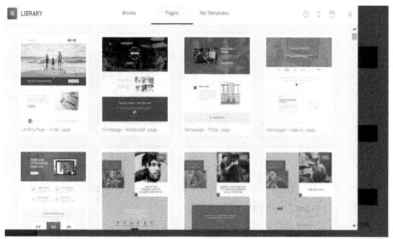

- Choose any design you want and click on insert. It's going to download and put it in there.

You can actually save this template and export it to any other website.

- Click on save and publish.
- Exit out of the page and go back to your dashboard.
- Click on templates again and go to saved templates.

You will see your template there, you can then export it to your computer and re-import it to any other website.

All the above steps are easily if you already know how to create templates on your own. This course is designed with newbie and non techy folks in mind. So to design your homepage, visit the homepage in your browser.

- Click edit with elementor.
- Click on add new section and choose one column from the list of columns.

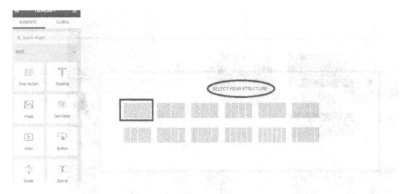

- Drag over an headings element from the list of widgets on the left hand side.

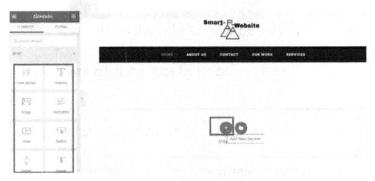

Type in the text you want and click align center below the text then click on style at the top.

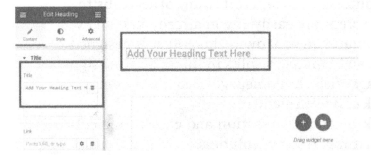

Change the color of the text and click on typography.

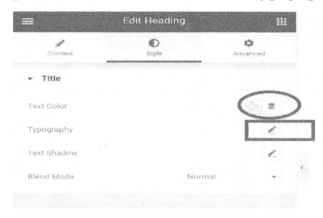

You can change the size of your text by making it big or small.
For the line spacing make it 4.7 or less depending on what you want.

- Click advance section at the top.

- Unlink the values for margin by clicking the link icon so that you can set different values for different margins.

- Make the top margin 150 0r 200, margin right 0, margin left 0 and margin bottom 0.
- Next, click the motion effect section and select animation for the text and set the animation delay and durations too.

- Go back to get more elements for the page by clicking on the widget menu at the top.

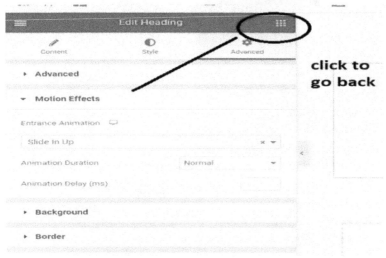

- Drag over a heading element and make it a subheading to the first heading text element .
- Type in the text on the left hand side and align center.
- Click on style to change the color. Make the color blue, red or black, change the font size to 19, make the weight 500.
- Click the element tab again to add inner section element (column element)

This time around we want to add two buttons to this columns side by side.

- Click on edit section to edit the section you just added i.e the two columns.

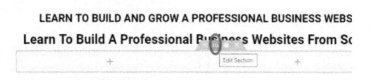

- Click advance and go to padding, unlink the values by clicking the link icon.

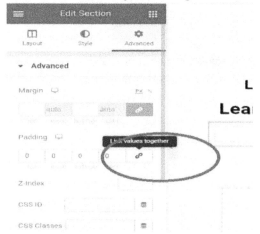

- Make the padding top 5 and the padding buttom 200.

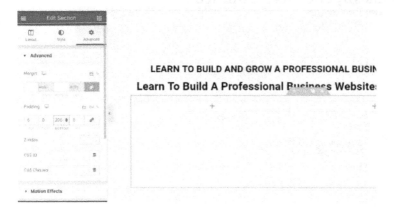

- Go back to element section, hold and drag the Button element in the first and second columns.

- Click on the first column and align the button to the right.
- Type in the text you want on the buttons eg click here, get started, visit the page etc. • Link it to a page.

- Click on style at the top and click typography.
- Under size, make it 13px (pixels).

- Change the text color to white or any color you want and change the background color to blue, red or black depending on your site color.
- Set the border radius to 5. That is how round you want the edges of the buttons to be and do not unlink the values.

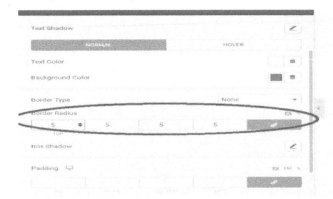

- Click the hover section and change the hover color to any color and you can also add animations to it when people click it, it will take effect.

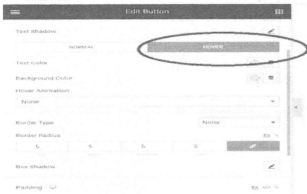

- Choose hover color for the background.
- Click on the second button column and type in your text.
- Click on style and change the text color.
- Click on typography to make the text size 13px and the border radius 5px.
- For border type, choose solid.
- For border radius choose 5px.
- For border color make It blue or white or any color.
- Scroll up and click on hover and change the

background color to sky blue or any color you want.

- Click on edit section icon at the top of the editing canvas, then click on style to choose background image from your desktop.

It is important to note that, there are four background types that you can use in your designs.

We have classic, gradient, videos and slideshows.

Classic is mostly used when you are adding an image to the background of a website. Gradient on the other hand is used when you are trying to blend two colors together and use them as backgrounds in your designs.

Video background type is used when you are adding a video to the background of your website. In this case, you will need to save your video to YouTube and then copy the URL or web address of the video to your designs and the video will start playing on the background.

And the last background type is the **slideshow** which is useful if you are adding a slideshow to the background of a website.

Now that we know the various background types that will have and since we are adding an image to the background;

For background type, select classic then click on choose image to select your background image from your desktop.

Scroll down after selecting your background image, set the position of the image to center-center or center-top as well as the size to be cover as shown in the image below.

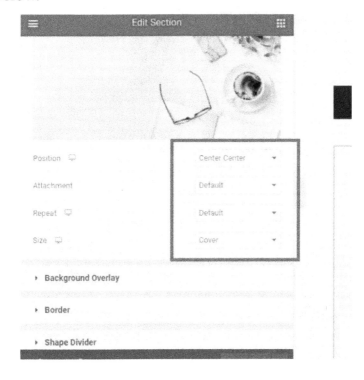

- Click on update and view your page in your browser.

Below is the image of our progress so far.

Check if the buttons are working by clicking them and by making sure they redirect to the appropriate link pages.

Note: If you notice your text is not very clear or bold on the background image, you can give the text a background color and to do that, click advance then go to background section to give the text a background color.

- Click on edit with elementor again from the top of your browser.
- Click on add new section icon below the page.
- Choose one column and add a text element.
- Type in your text and align it center.
- Click on style at the top to change the color to your choice color.
- Click on typography below the text color and set the size to 30 and for the weight, make it 300 or 400.
- Click advance at the top.
- Unlink the margin values to be able to add different values. This will create some spaces between the section at the top and the second section as shown in the image below.

- Make the margin top and margin bottom 40 or 50 i.e the same value.
- Add another section and choose three columns.
- Drag in the image element, drag in the heading element at the top of it and the text element below it as well as the button element below the text element in the same section as shown in the image below.

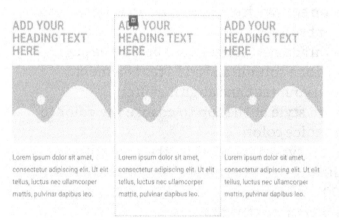

- Go to the first column and click the heading element, type in your heading texts (Our services, our work, about us etc.) on the left hand side of the page and align it to the center.
- Click on the image element to add your image by choosing an image from your desktop.
- Click on the text element section, add in some

texts about your business or niche then click advance, unlink the values for padding, add 20 to the left and right padding boxes.

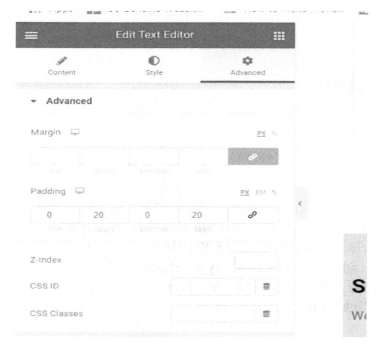

- Click the buttons you added to the bottom of the text element, type in the text for the button element, align it center and link the text to a page.
- Click on style to change the text color and the background color.

- Click on typography, change the size to 12px and change the weight to 500 or less.
- Click advance, for border type, choose solid, for border radius make it 6 and choose hover color by clicking the hover section.

Now that we are done editing the first column, the next thing we are going to do is to duplicate this column twice, making the total columns 5. To do that, hover over the edit column button and click the duplicate button twice.

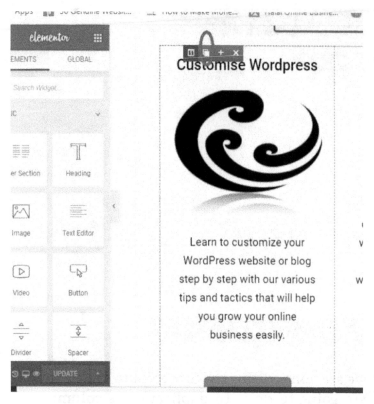

- Delete the last two of the columns sections so that you can be left with three columns.
- Change the heading texts, the images, the text elements contents and the buttons texts for the duplicated columns.
- Click on update then view your progress.

Note: The image icons you see above can be gotten from logo maker website. Use the training on how to use the platform to get your images downloaded. You can type in something like ocean, float, writing, to get them displayed.

- Click on edit with elementor again to go back.
- Scroll down and add new section.
- Choose two columns from the list.

What we want to do is to change the background color of the section. To do that click on edit section button.

- Click on style at the top, for background type choose classic and make the color light grey.

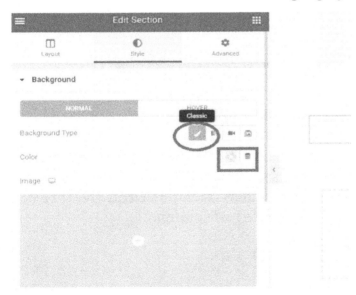

- Click advance, unlink the value for margin and set the margin top to 50.
- Unlink the value for padding also and set the padding top and bottom to 40.

This will make our column box to be a little bit bigger.

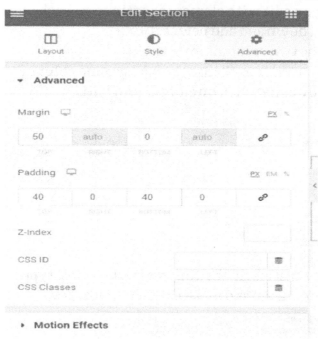

- Drag in heading element in the first column and change the title to our work or our services.
- Click on style and click typography.
- Set the size to 30, scroll down to line height and set it to 0.8.
- Click advance, unlink the values under margin and set the margin top to 20.
- Click on add widget menu and add the text element under the first column.

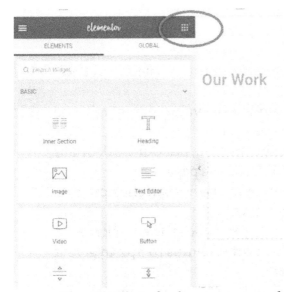

- Give a little info about your work or services.
- Click on add element button again, drag and drop the inner section element on the second column.

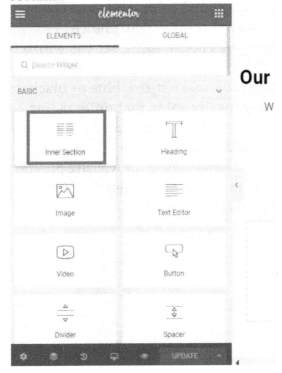

What we are trying to do is to put two buttons there side by side.

- Click edit column from top of the second column.
- Click advance, unlink the values for margin and set the margin top to 28.
- For text on the first button, put our work or our services then link it to the page.
- Align the button to the right then click on style and go to typography.
- Set the size to 15px, choose the background color and set the border radius to 5px to give it rounded edges.
- For the second button, type in your text e.g view our work and change the link to our work.
- Click on style and click typography.
- Set the size to 15px, change the text color.
- Make the background color white and transparent or choose any color of your choice.
- For border type choose solid, set the width to 2px.
- For border color, make it red, blue or black depending on your site color, for border radius, set it to 5px and set padding to 10px
- Change the hover color for text and button.
- Click on update and view your website progress.
- Now, you need to view your website on the mobile to see how its looks.

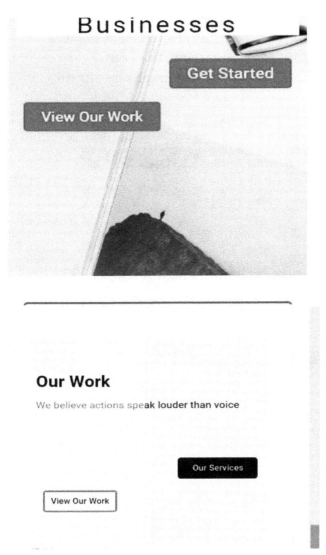

You can see that some of the buttons are not aligned and that is the more reason why we need to create the mobile version of our website.

Trust me, this single act will distinguish you from the rest. Most web designers don't pay attention to how their websites look on mobile phones which is where most users are engaged with their contents.

To do that, duplicate the section that has issues. That

will make the section to appear twice.

Let's make the first section our desktop version and the duplicated section our mobile version. then scroll down to edit the second section which is going to be our mobile version.

- Click on the headline then click on style by the left hand side.

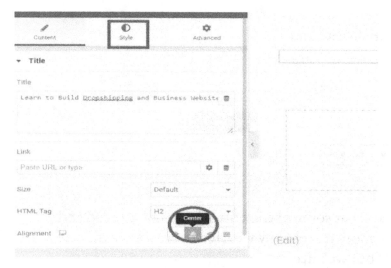

- Click on typography and reduce the font size to half of the size on the desktop version.
- Click on the two buttons one after the other and align them to the center.

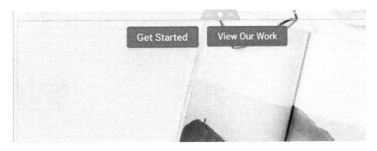

Now, we need to indicate which one is the desktop version and which one is the mobile section. What we need to do is to hide the mobile version on the desktop version as well as hide the desktop version on the mobile version.

To do that, go to the desktop version and click the edit section button.

LEARN TO BUILD AND GROW A PROFESSIONAL BUSINESS WEBS

Learn To Build A Professional Business Websites From Sc

Edit Section

- Go to advance on the left hand side.
- Scroll down and click on responsive. • Enable the button that says "hide on mobile".

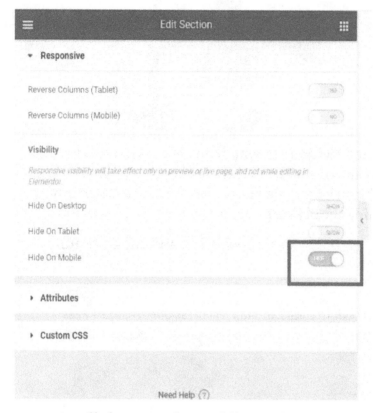

- Scroll down to the mobile version · Click edit section button.
- Click advance and go to responsive.
- Enable the buttons that says "hide on desktop" and "hide on tablet".
- Click on update then view the webistes on both mobile and desktop.

Below is how the mobile version looks on my mobile phone.

Our Work

We believe actions speak louder than voice

You can see that the title and the buttons are now aligned and the website is looking great.

Now we are done creating the mobile and the desktop version of our homepage. Well done so far!

CHAPTER 4, MODULE 5
HOW TO CUSTOMIZE THE ABOUT US PAGE AND OUR WORK PAGE.

To edit and customize the about us page, click on the page in the navigation bar from your browser. You will need to get rid of the title and the sidebar on that page first.

Remember the title toggle plugin we installed earlier? It will help us get rid of the about us title written on the screen and the sidebar on the right hand side.

To do that, click on edit page at the top.

- Scroll down to layout settings.
- Select no sidebar layout and check the hide title box.
- Scroll up and click on update.

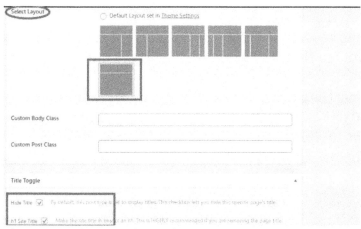

And now, we have a clean about us page to start customizing as shown in the image below.

Now that our about us page is free of the site title and sidebar then we are good to go.

- Click on edit page at the top.
- Click edit with elementor.
- It will redirect you to elementor design interface.
- Click on add new section.

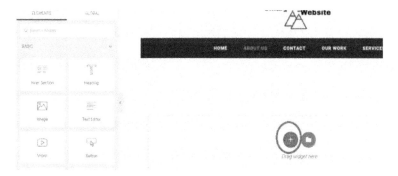

What we want to do is to add a background image and

some text on the image.

We are going to choose three columns layout from the list of layouts so that the text can be fix to the middle or one side.

Hold and drag the three columns you choose and adjust it to 30|40|30 or 40|30|30 depending on where your face is facing in the image you are going to be adding as show in the image below.

- Click the edit section button.
- Click style at the top left of the page.
- Scroll down to background and make sure is on classic then choose the background image and click insert media.

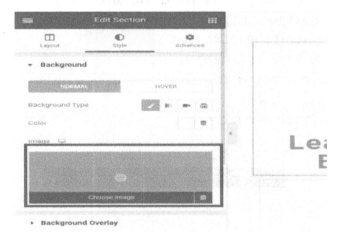

Scroll down a bit to position and set it to center-center and under size choose cover.

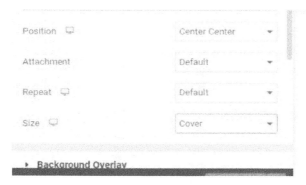

You will notice that the image is still not tall enough so we need to add some content.

- Click the widgets menu and choose a text editor element.

In my own case, I will be placing the text editor element in the first column (i.e 40|30|30) because of where am facing in the image.

- Type in your text and align it center.
- Choose your text color and click on typography.
- Make the text size 20 or 23
- Make the weight of the text 300 or 400 depending on how bold or thin you want the text to be.

- Click advance at the top.
- Unlink the values for margin. Set the margin top to 125 and the margin bottom to 375 or 380.

This will give it more space and we can actually see more of our background image.

- Scroll down to background section and make sure the background type is set to classic and make the background color white so that we can see the text easily.

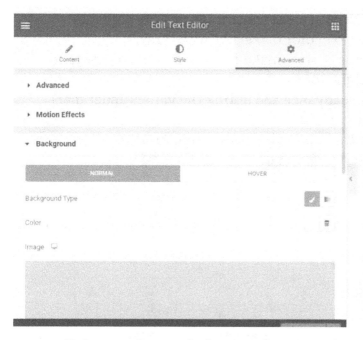

- Click on update and view your progress in your browser.

Making the column three helps us to position the text properly.
- Click edit with elementor again to continue editing.
- Click on add new section and choose three columns.
- Hold and drag the columns until you are able to position it to 20|60|20.

What we want to do is that we want to type in a brief introduction about us or our company at the middle column.
- Click the add widget menu at the top.
- Drag in a text element to the middle column and type a little introduction about yourself or what your business is all about.
- Highlight the text and click align center.

- Click on style at the top and go to typography.
- For text color make it black or grey.
- For text size, make it 24px and make the font weight 400.
- Click advance and unlink the values under margin.
- Set the top and bottom margin to 100.

- Click on update then view your progress in your browser.

View it on mobile to know if you need to adjust anything by creating the mobile version of the page.

Note: If you feel like adding more pictures of yourself or some event photos you will like to share, then click edit with elementor and click add new section again. Choose three columns and drag in the image element then add your images.

Now we are done editing the about us page.

HOW TO CUSTOMIZE THE OUR WORK PAGE.

To edit our work page, click edit page and get rid of the title and sidebar following our previous instruction on how to do that.

- Click on edit with elementor and add new section.
- Choose three columns from the options.

- Hold and drag the column and set it to 20|60|20.
- Click on the add widget to add the text element and place it at the center column.
- Type in some quotes about your business.
- E.g web design quotes, yoga quotes, food quotes etc. Just search for quotes about your business online and type it in the middle column.
- Align the text to the center and click on style at the top.
- Click on the text color box to change the text color to grey and click on typography.
- For font size make it 28px, make weight 300 and for letter spacing, make it 2px.
- Scroll up and click on advance.
- Unlink the margin values and set the top and bottom margin to 150.
- Duplicate this section by clicking the duplicate button.

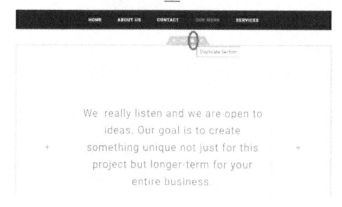

- Type in another business quote, align it center.
- Click add new section in between the two sections you duplicated. You can do that on top of the second section by clicking the plus button.

We really listen and we are open to
ideas. Our goal is to create
+ something unique not just for this +
project but longer-term for your
entire business.

What we want to do is to add images in between them. i.e. One quote follows by an image, another quote follows by another image.

- Click to add new section with the plus button between the two sections carrying the quotes and choose one column.
- Drag in the spacer element and make the size 400px.

- Click on style and click background type classic then choose the image on your computer.
- For image position, make it center-center and for size make it cover.
- Duplicate this section and place the image at the appropriate place.
- Click on update and view our work page in your browser.

Our goal is to create something unique not just for this project but longer-term for your entire business.

CHAPTER 5, MODULE 6.
HOW TO CUSTOMIZE THE CONTACT PAGE
AND THE SERVICES PAGE

What we need to do under contact page customization is that, we need to add a map, a contact form and an image (optional).

First of all, let's get rid of the title and the sidebar on our contact page following the previous lesson on how to do that.

- Click on edit page.
- Click edit with elementor.
- Click on add new section and choose one column.
- Drag in the google maps element from the list of elements.

You can change the default address by typing in your location address.

Now when you look at the map carefully, you can see that there is a little bit of spaces at the side and at the top. To get rid of that, click on edit section and under content width, set it to full width and under column gap, choose no gap and that should get rid of the spaces on the two sides of the map.

As for the space at the top, leave it, the way it is cause is not going to show in your browser so don't worry about it.

The next thing we are going to do is to add new section and choose two columns type with the left column being much bigger.

- Add new element button (text editor) and type in your email address and phone number.
- Click advance, unlink the value for margin and put 15px for the top and the bottom margins.
- Add an image element under the first column and add an image which is optional.

Next, we will need to add a contact form to the second column and to do that we are going to install a plugin called contact form 7.

Follow the previous lesson on how to install and activate a plugin.

- Click on contact on the left hand side of your dashboard after installing and activating the plugin.
- Click on contact forms to see the list of contact forms you have there.

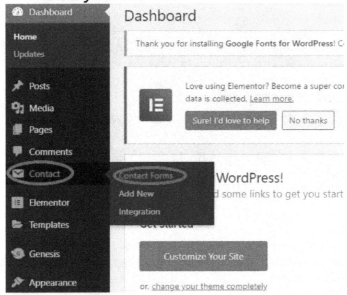

- Click on contact form 1.
- Click on mail to see if you have the right e-mail address in there.

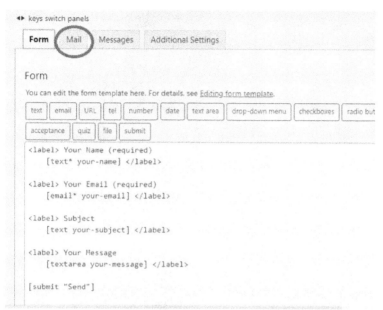

If you are sure everything is correct, then copy the short-code and go back to your elementor editing page by clicking edit with elementor again

- Drag in the shortcode element into the second column.
- Paste the code you copy from contact form 7 plugin and click apply.

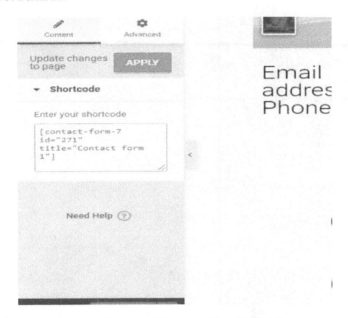

And your contact form will start displaying.

- Click on the contact form and click advance.
- Unlink the value for margin then make the top and the bottom margin 15px.
- Click on update and view your contact page in your browser.

Now we are done editing the contact page.

HOW TO CUSTOMIZE THE SERVICES PAGE.

To start customizing our services page, just like we have done for the rest of the pages, we will need to get rid of the title and the sidebar then click edit with elementor. In customizing the services page, we are going to be putting our services side by side some images. So to do that, click on add new section and choose two columns.

- Click on edit column at the top of the page.
- Click advance, unlink the padding values.
- Make the top and bottom padding 30.
- Click on add widget menu and add a heading

element.
- Change the text by typing in your own. • Change the text color to black or grey • Click on style and go to typography.
- For font size make it 38 and make the width 300.
- Click advance, unlink the values for margin and set top margin to 25.
- Click add widget button.
- Drag in a text editor element and change the text by giving a little introduction about your business or the product that you offer.
- Hold and drag the image button to the right column, choose the image from your desktop.
- Click the duplicate button to duplicate the section.
- Change the heading text, the body text as well as add another image to the right column.

What I want us to do is to add a call to action at the bottom of our services page just like we have on the home page as shown in the image below.

Instead of recreating this section on the services page, we can just visit the home page and save the desktop and the mobile version of this section as templates and insert it into the services page we are editing. To do that, visit the homepage of the website you are building in your browser.
- Click edit with elementor.
- Scroll down to the desktop version of the call to action buttons.
- Right click on the edit section icon and choose

save as template or click the save icon.

- Name the template and click on save.

- Right click on the edit section icon on the mobile version and choose save as template or click the save icon.
- Give it a name and click save.

Go back to the services page and click edit with elementor.

- Click on add template icon.

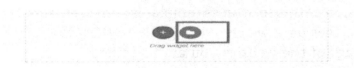

You will be redirected to elementor inbuilt templates.

- Click on my template at the top to see your saved template.

- Click on insert for the desktop version.
- Repeat the step and click insert for the mobile version too.

You can also click on each button to change the texts and the links on the buttons if you want.

- Click on update then view our page.

The next thing we are going to do is to customize the footer section of our website.

CHAPTER 6, MODULE 7.
HOW TO CUSTOMIZE THE FOOTER SECTION
OF YOUR WEBSITE

The footer is the bottom section of any website just like we have the header being the top of any website.

What we are going to do in the footer area is that we are going to design our own footer section and replace it with the default footer on the website.

First of all, let's visit our footer area at the backend. To do that, click on customize then click on theme settings.

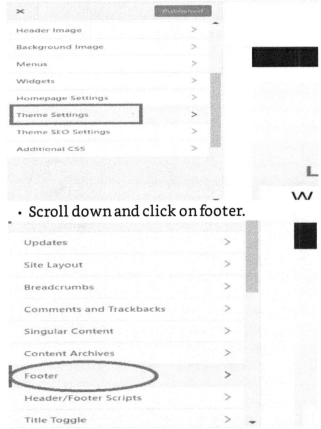

• Scroll down and click on footer.

The codes holding the footer area will be displayed on the left hand side of the page. When you scroll down to the footer area, you will be able to see the corresponding texts at the bottom of every page.

[footer_copyright before="Copyright "]·
[footer_childtheme_link before="" after="
on"] [footer_genesis_link url="https://
www.studiopress.com/" before=""]·
[footer_wordpress_link]·[footer_loginout]

- Click to go back to your dashboard.
- Click on customize again and go to menu.
- Click on create new menu and name it footer.

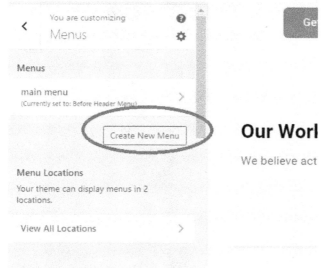

- Click on next and select items for the menu by clicking the plus icons.

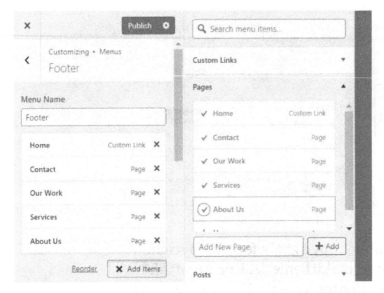

- Click on publish at the top.

The next thing we are going to do is to create a template for the footer and to do that, we are going to need a plugin called Elementor Header Footer and Block.

Go over to your plugin section, search for the plugin, install it and activate it.

- Go back to your dashboard.
- Click on appearance and click on the plugin you just installed.

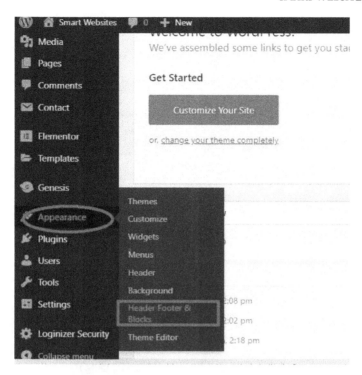

- Click on add new at the top.

- Name the template and choose the type of template you want to create.

- Choose where to display the template (Entire site)

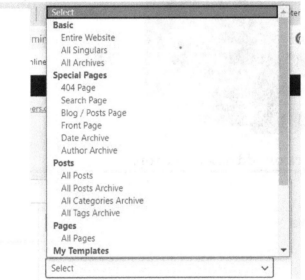

- Click the dropdown button to pick a user rule.
- Check the small box below it and click on publish.

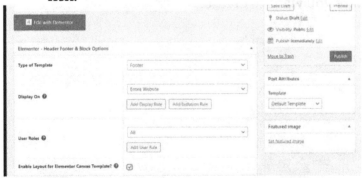

- Click edit with elementor at the top. This will open elementor editing canvas page.

You can add an already created template or start from scratch.
To start from scratch, click the edit section icon and choose three columns.

What we want to do is that we want to put in our logo, navigation menu and social media icons.

- Click on edit section at the top.
- For content width make it full width.
- Enable the stretch section by clicking "Yes"
- Set the column position to middle and the minimum height to 300 0r 400.

- Click advance and for margin, let's make it zero for top and bottom.
- Click on style and choose classic as the background type.
- Scroll down to add a background image or choose a background color like grey or black.
- For position of the image, make it top-center or bottom-right and for size, make it cover.
- Click the add element section to add some elements.
- Drag in the copyright icon in the first column and the image icon.
- Put in your URL in the copyright link and add your logo in the image element then set the custom size of the image to 30x30 and click apply. Also type in your URL in the image link to link to your homepage.
- Click advance and unlink the value for margin then make margin top 20.
- Drag in social media icons in the second column and link to your social media accounts.

- Click on style and under typography, make the size 19px, change the padding to 0.6 and spacing to 9px.

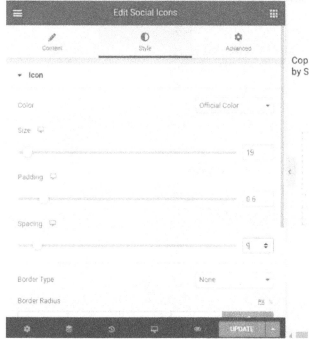

- Drag in the navigation menu icon in the third column, choose the footer menu from the left hand side.

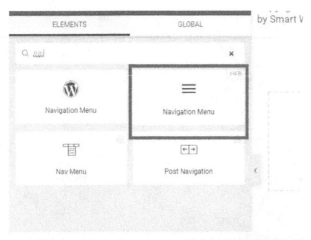

by Smart V

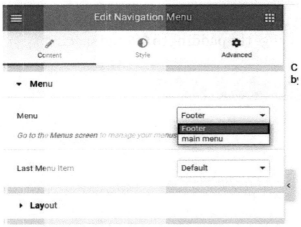

C
b

- For position, let's make it right.
- Click advance, unlink the values for margin and make the right margin 40px.

- Click on publish or update at the bottom and reload your website.

And here is the image of what we just designed below.

However, viewing this design on the mobile version, doesn't look great.

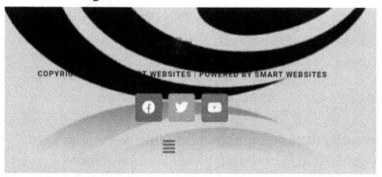

So, we would need to create the mobile version of our footer separately.

To do that, right click on the edit section icon and choose duplicate.

- Click advance and go to responsive section.
- Enable the button that says "hide on mobile" then click update.

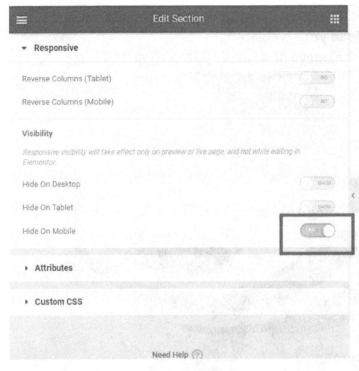

Go to the duplicate section, depending on the type of image you uploaded, in my own case I will be removing the image completely leaving only the background color. You can try changing the position of your image to either bottom-right or bottom-left.

- Interchange the first and the third column contents by pointing your cursor to each pencil icon then holding and dragging each element to where you want.

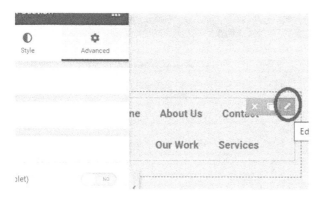

Click advance and go to responsive section.
Enable "hide on tablet and hide on desktop buttons"

- Click on update and view your website in the browser.
- Click on all the links and buttons to make sure they are all working properly.

And we are done creating our websites and ready to start designing for clients!

Header, Footer & Blocks plugin is an amazing addon from elementor. You can also customize your header and create blocks with this plugin.

Elementor plugin is very powerful in creating amazing website designs. It is one of the best page builders out there that you can use to transform the look of any website or blog. While the free version of elementor gives you access to customize some part of your website, the PRO version of elementor gives you full access to all your site customization. Elementor Pro offers many more professionally made templates and blocks that can be easily customized to create stunning websites. With the Pro version, you can create pages featuring slides, animated headlines, custom sidebars, forms and other important features.

You can check out the pro version here.

Your website is ready, CONGRATULATIONS!

So, How Do You Start Creating Websites for Clients in Minutes?

Creating multiple websites in minutes is actually possible once you have all your website templates handy and ready to use for future designs.

To save our website designs as templates, we would need to save each page, block or sections that we have customized with elementor page builder as templates including the header or footer.

To do that, go to the page, block or any section you will like to save as template and click edit with elementor.

- Click on the save options button at the bottom of elementor page editor and choose save as template from the options.

- Give the template a name base on the page you are saving as template like Homepage, contact, our work, services or footer etc.

- Click on save.

This is the process you follow to save all your customized pages, blocks or sections as templates after which you can then download or export them in to your computer.

To access your saved template, scroll down and click on the add template button.

Here, you will be presented with three options- Blocks, pages and my templates.

Click on my templates to access all your saved templates.

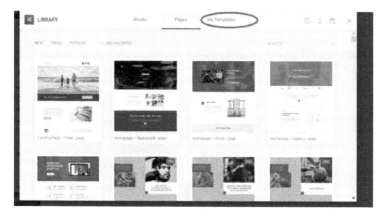

- Click on the three dots in front of the template you wish to download and choose export, as shown in the image below.

- Hover over the three dots in front of each saved templates and export them on to your computer or desktop

- Create a folder on your desktop to keep all your exported templates in one place.

To reuse these templates on another website, you will need to repeat our previous steps of getting a domain name and hosting as well as installing WordPress. Or maybe you wish to redesign or rebrand an old website.

All you have to do is to install your theme, install elementor plugin, install header footer & blocks plugin, create your website pages as well as your navigation menus. Visit each page you created, choose to edit with elem-

entor and this will take you to elementor editing interface or canvas.

- Click the add template icon.

You will be redirected to a page as shown in the image
below.

- Click the import button at the top of the page.
- Choose the template you need from your computer by clicking the select file button.

This will take you to the folder where all your templates

are saved.

- Choose the file and click on open.

And viola, one of your website's pages is ready!

You may choose to customize this page or section further by changing the colors, font sizes, adjusting the margins or padding as well as working on the background image to suite the requirements of your clients.

Repeat these steps to import all your pages or designs into the new project you are working on and begin to customize to your taste then position yourself as a Professional Website designer.

This brings us to the end of this training, I hope it helps you in creating amazing websites.

To your success!

About Me

Hello and welcome to the Training "Smart Websites in Minutes!"

My name is Modupe Salmat. I am an Online Entrepreneur, Full-time Blogger and a WordPress/Ecommerce expert. I work Online fulltime for a living and I love teaching people how to do the same via some of my life changing trainings and online courses. I created this training manual to show people how easy it is to build professional websites for clients using WordPress and you can only achieve your aim of purchasing this material if you digest it thoroughly and make the best use of it.

I hope you enjoy it

ABOUT THE AUTHOR

Modupe Salmat

Modupe Salmat is an online entrepreneur and a web designer. She loves helping people with her skills and knowledge in teaching them how to make passive income online via various online courses and training